BEGINNING
VOLLEYBALL

WILLIAM T. ODENEAL
*State University College
of New York, New Paltz*

HARRY E. WILSON
United States Volleyball Association

WADSWORTH PUBLISHING COMPANY, INC.
Belmont, California

L.C. Cat. Card No.: 61-15841

Printed in the United States of America

Eighth printing: September 1966

CONTENTS

VALUES

The speed of a spiked volleyball is purported to be in excess of 100 miles an hour. Considering the speed of baseball pitcher Bob Feller's fast ball at 94 miles an hour as a comparison, it is obvious that it is quite a task to keep a volleyball in play and then return it to the opponent at the same speed. Volleyball, when played well, is a fast, vigorous game.

Volleyball brings into use all of the large muscle groups, requires natural body movements, and demands speed, coordination, and strength for a good game. Dr. J. L. Rudd of Boston, Massachusetts, in his medical opinion on the value of volleyball, stated that "for the individual who does his regular volleyball playing there is a sufficient amount of energy expended and conditioning gained so that, if he is called upon to exert himself in an emergency, he could do so without undue strain on muscles of extremities, back, or heart."

A late afternoon game of volleyball can do much to dispel nervousness, dullness, and spiritual depression. Volleyball is one of the few competitive games that the average person can play for exercise, relaxation, and fun, or the active athlete can play for a strenuous workout. The game requires what all athletes like in a game: skill, endurance, coordination, physical tension, and much muscular activity. The average player receives most of these physiological benefits also, even though he plays mostly for fun.

Volleyball is one of the truly amateur sports; the spirit of amateurism always prevails. Volleyball players play the game for fun and exercise. Tournaments exhibit the absence of booing and bad conduct. There is a strong spirit of moral conduct evident when a player raises his hand in a tournament to admit touching a ball that the referee and spectators did not know was touched. There is no rule that requires a player to admit that he touched the ball that went out of bounds. Yet, this test of high moral fiber and human conduct is a tradition of the game that was developed in 1895 and has existed down through the years.

Although there are rapid changes in height, weight, strength, speed, endurance, and coordination from the junior high school age to the high school age, volleyball is the ideal game for school years. Care should be exercised that demands of overstrenuous participation are not made on students in this age bracket, especially in highly competitive sports. Volleyball is easily geared to the abilities of students of this age. College level volleyball should stress the *fundamental skills* of the activities taught in junior and senior high school because, although students entering college may have sufficient interest, they usually are not thoroughly grounded in the fundamental skills of a wide variety of activities. Most college students want to participate in recreational sports where there is much activity and where there is carry-over value. Volleyball is a game designed for recreation and leisure-time activities as well as for conditioning, and fits excellently into the college program. It also provides the opportunity for the formation of the friendships and group loyalties that are important in campus life. The game is one of the most popular intramural sports in colleges and universities.

SUMMARY

Most physical educators or volleyball players will agree that volleyball has the following benefits:

1. It has good carry-over value—can be played for a lifetime.
2. It is a game for all ages and both sexes.
3. It provides fun for most participants.
4. It is a good conditioner—develops physical fitness.
5. It develops teamwork.
6. Volleyball is a good coeducational activity.
7. It is a year-round game that can be played indoors and outdoors.
8. It develops friendships through playing together.
9. Little space is necessary for play, making the game widely available for large numbers of participants.
10. There is little expense involved.

Volleyball is an extremely desirable sport by any standard of evaluation of the various activities in a physical education or recreation program. The game serves to develop organic power; it calls for a high degree of neuromuscular coordination; and it is one of the most popular of all leisure-time activity games. A most important aspect of the game is that it stresses the importance of cooperative effort, which is the key to developing good neighbors and citizens.

The Origin of the Game

While physical director at Holyoke (Mass.) YMCA, William Morgan had an idea for a new indoor game. He stretched across the gym a net 6 feet 6 inches high and used the sides of the gym as boundaries. For a ball he used the bladder from a ball made by a local sporting goods store. The object of the game was to hit or bat the ball back and forth over the net with the hands. The game began with a serve over the net. Each server was allowed three "outs" before the opposing team was permitted to serve. An out resulted when the ball landed out of bounds or hit the floor after more than one bounce. Morgan incorporated elements of tennis, baseball, and handball into his game.

As Physical Director at the Holyoke YMCA, Morgan found that the game of basketball was too strenuous for his noon-day class of businessmen. He needed a game for the older men that was not too vigorous, yet a game that would afford some relaxation and recreation. Thus, Mr. Morgan's ideas and experiences on the gym floor with his noon-day classes produced a new game suitable not only for his classes but for the world.

At a YMCA Sports Conference at Springfield College in 1896, Mr. Morgan presented his game publicly. The name given to the game was *Mintonette*. After watching the game, Dr. A. T. Halstead, a faculty member of Springfield College, recommended the name *Volleyball* because of the nature of the game. Following this conference, the *Journal of the YMCA* presented the first comprehensive coverage of the game, including a description of the rules, and Mr. Morgan's report to the conference.

Other YMCA men adopted the game. Late in 1896 W. E. Day introduced this new sport at Dayton, Ohio. He and his assistants revised the rules according to their experience with the game in their physical training classes. As a result, in 1900 the Physical Directors' Society of the YMCA adopted a set of rules. They raised the net to

4

7 feet 6 inches, eliminated the first bounce and the innings, tried to standardize the ball handling, and set twenty-one points to constitute a game. In 1912 this same society formulated the fifteen-point game, introduced rotation of players, made a serve touching the net a side-out, and introduced the two-game match.

In June, 1907, at the first annual convention of the Playground of America (now the National Recreation Association), volleyball was presented as one of the most popular out-of-door games.

Volleyball Growth Tremendous

In 1915 the education profession as a whole took note of the value of volleyball as a team sport and recommended its use in the athletic program along with baseball, basketball, and football. Under the direction of George J. Fisher, YMCA workers stressed volleyball in the Armed Forces during World War I; the game was enthusiastically received, and after the war, many of the former servicemen continued to play the game. On April 28, 1922, twenty-three YMCA teams from eleven states and Canada played in the first National YMCA Championship held in Brooklyn, New York. Pittsburgh YMCA was the winner.

Under the leadership of A. P. Idell, during the early 1920's, many changes in the rules were introduced. During this period the modern net and ball were developed and the court dimensions were set at 30 feet by 60 feet.

In 1928 the United States Volleyball Association (hereafter referred to as the USVBA) was organized primarily to administer and coordinate volleyball rules on a national scale and to create a national open tournament. The former name of this organization was The Volleyball Rules Committee of the YMCA.

During the 1930's recreational sports progressed greatly; through the Works Progress Administration, about $500,000,000 was spent on 3,700 recreational buildings, 888 parks, 1,500 athletic fields, and many other facilities. Schools learned the values of recreation; soon most schools and recreational leaders agreed that volleyball was one of their most popular sports.

During the 1940's there was even greater interest in volleyball. The Golden Anniversary year, 1945, featured more written articles about volleyball than any year in its entire history. In 1946 the leaders in volleyball were recognized by the USVBA. Also in 1946, in an annual recreational study, it was quoted that volleyball ranked fifth among team sports being promoted and organized. In 1947 there were 13,481 volleyballs manufactured; in 1953, there were 21,751. In 1949 the USVBA sponsored the first National Collegiate and National Women's Open Tournament. In 1952 the National Armed Forces Tournament was presented along with the National YMCA, Open, Veterans, and the above-mentioned tournaments.

In 1958 the United States Volleyball Association was given official jurisdiction over the game in the United States for Olympic games and Pan American games competition. In 1958 the women's athletic division of the American Association for Health, Physical Education and Recreation revised their rules to coincide with the women's rules of the USVBA. The rule book also featured a college section in the official guide in the 1950's.

Originally, it was through the efforts of the YMCA that the game of volleyball was spread throughout the world; however, the Armed Forces of the United States must be recognized as having been responsible for tremendous promotion of the game both abroad and at home. It is apparent with the inclusion of volleyball in the Olympic games that the future emphasis should come from schools and colleges. And it is through the development of leagues and in competition that we are to produce champions and representatives for the United States against foreign competition.

Volleyball is now a fast, rigorous game played by top athletes. The game has progressed from a slow, helter-skelter, bat-the-ball-over-the-net-at-any-cost game, to a deliberate, accurate, and exciting game. The serve has been developed from a lob to a hard, well-placed ball. Passing has changed from pushing or throwing the ball over the net to deliberate, accurate passing involving a high degree of skilled teamwork.

Volleyball—International Game

According to Dr. Hui Ching Lu, in her doctoral dissertation, "Volleyball Around the World," volleyball is played in more than sixty countries and by more than fifty million people each year. In such countries as Rumania, Russia, France, Czechoslovakia, Japan, Mexico, and Brazil, championship matches draw crowds rivaling and many times exceeding those at football and basketball games in the United States. Volleyball is ranked third in the world as a recreational team sport and in at least twenty-five countries it is rated the leading competitive sport. In 1956 the World Volleyball Championships in Paris drew teams from twenty-seven countries and filled the *Palais des Sports* on several occasions with crowds of twenty-five thousand people. In Japan and in Russia, it is not uncommon to see forty thousand people watching championship volleyball.

An International Volleyball Federation has full-time officers and offices in Paris, France. It is composed of sixty-two countries and is the international governing body of volleyball. This group is responsible for publishing the international rules and promotion of the annual world's volleyball championships.

EQUIPMENT

THE COURT

Volleyball is played on a court 60 feet long and 30 feet wide measured to the outer edges of the boundary lines, which are 2 inches wide (Illus. 1). A line 2 inches wide is marked across the center of the playing surface to separate the courts. The service areas are marked by two lines 6 inches long extended from the side lines. A back position spiking line (also called the restraining line) is drawn

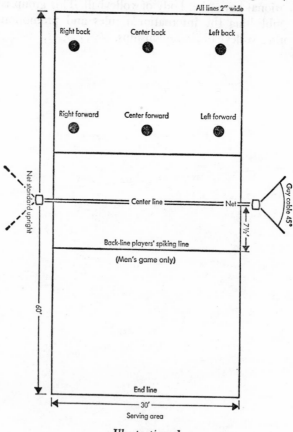

All lines 2" wide

Right back   Center back   Left back

Right forward   Center forward   Left forward

Net standard upright

Center line ———— Net

Guy cable 45°

7½'

Back-line players' spiking line

(Men's game only)

60'

End line

30'

Serving area

Illustration 1

across each court from side line to side line, 7½ feet from and parallel to the middle of the center line. The purpose of this line is to prevent extremely tall players from coming to the net to spike the ball on every play. A back line player may spike the ball, if he remains on or behind this spiking line.

The court is divided by a net, the top of which is 8 feet from the floor for college men and open play. For college women and open play, the net is 7 feet 4½ inches from the floor. For high school boys the net is 7 feet 6 inches from the floor, and for high school girls the net is 7 feet from the floor. The net is 32 feet long, 3 feet wide, with a 4-inch square mesh of number 30 thread. It is bound top, ends, and bottom with a ¼-inch manila rope. A double thickness of white canvas 2 inches wide is sewn to the top, and through this is run a ¼-inch cable. The ultimate strength of the cable is 7,000 pounds. On one end it is drawn by a ratchet or tightening device to eliminate variation in net height. A 2-inch vertical marker (generally of masking or adhesive tape) is placed on the net directly above the side lines to indicate the sides of the court. The net is stretched by four corners between uprights or standards. The bottom of the net is drawn taut by ropes anchoring the lower corners. Guy wires, standards, or other supports are built to withstand a lateral working stress of 2,000 pounds.

There is, generally, a need for additional supports to the outside of the standards because the floor supports that hold them are not strong enough to withstand the 2,000 pounds of lateral working stress that is required. These additional side supports (usually ¼-inch guy wire cables) run from the top of the standard and are attached either to a wall or to the floor, generally at a 45-degree angle from the standards so as not to interfere with the referee's vision and to prevent lateral motion of the net.

OUTDOOR COURTS

When outdoor courts are constructed in camps, at beaches, playgrounds, or parks, and painted 2-inch lines are not practical, boundaries may be made of rope, strips of cloth, or flat metal strips nailed to the ground at the corners beneath the net. In the event marble dust is used, a shallow trench should be dug to contain the dust and make it more lasting.

THE REFEREE'S STAND

The referee's stand and standards for competitive play are to be erected at least 3 feet away from the side lines so that players will not run into them during play. The referee's stand, with a floor 3 feet by 4 feet, is placed at one end of the net so that the top of the stand is 8 feet 3 inches from the floor so that the referee's head may be 2–3 feet above the net. In Illustration 2, the net is shown attached to a referee's stand.

THE SCOREBOARD

A scoreboard that is visible to spectators, players, and officials should be used to show the visitor's score and the home score. The scoreboard may be either manual or electric.

For class play, numbers from 1 to 20 may be painted on separate linoleum or cardboard sheets and attached to a board placed either on the referee's stand or scorer's table. Each time a score is made a sheet is turned to expose the score.

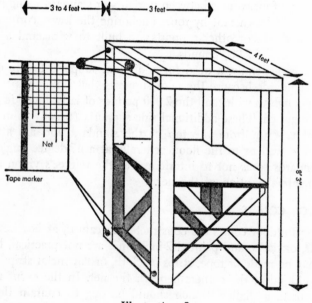

Illustration 2

THE NET

Illustration 3 shows the net and its attachments. The ¼-inch cable that runs through the top of the net has loops in both ends. To each loop is attached a double harness snap. One harness snap is secured to an eye hook on one standard. The other snap is secured to a loop of cable that runs through a pulley attached to the top of the other standard. Both eye hook and pulley are 8 feet 2 inches from the floor. This short piece of cable runs through the pulley and connects to a ratchet, which is fastened to the standard about 4 feet from the floor. The bottom of the net on both sides is secured to a small loop 3½ feet from the floor on both standards. The pull of the bottom rope controls the height of the net; therefore the rope should be looped around the standard for quick removal rather than tied in a knot.

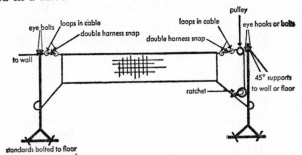

Illustration 3

In the event two or more nets are to be put up side by side, the cable support from one standard is attached directly to the next standard (which may allow some lateral movement of the net). If the space between standards is more than 15 feet, the supports should be secured to floor plates.

Most indoor gymnasiums use the regulation standard, which is equipped with attachments for the nets and has screws in the base that secure it to the floor plates. The biggest problem in most gymnasiums, however, is the lack of floor plates for the standards. When there are no floor plates the standards can be supported by ropes or cables anchored to the walls. Many schools use posts anchored to a cement-filled automobile tire. Ropes or cables attached to the top of the standard are anchored to the wall to keep the net taut. This arrangement allows lateral motion and some sag of the net, but is satisfactory for class play.

It is important that strong nets and cable be used in official games. The supports, if not sturdy, will not keep the net tight and at the proper height; thus, many fouls and violations will occur because the net will sag and sway into the players. Inexpensive nets made of cotton and substandard thread can be purchased from any sporting goods store. These nets are not bound at the top, do not have ropes at the top and bottom, and will sag when erected.

If the net is to be left overnight, the tension must be released to avoid overstretching. Outside nets should be taken down, folded, and stored after each day's play.

When the game is played by young children, the net is lowered to 1 foot above the raised hand of the average child. With the net low enough for a child to achieve success, he enjoys the game and wants to continue playing because he can master the basic fundamentals of the game.

THE BALL

The official game is played with a spherical ball having a rubber bladder, a twelve-piece laceless leather case or a rubber case, not less than 26 inches nor more than 27 inches in circumference, and weighing not less than 9 nor more than 10 ounces (for women, not less than 7 nor more than 9 ounces). The leather ball carries air pressure of not less than 7 nor more than 8 pounds; the rubber ball carries not less than 5 nor more than 7 pounds of pressure.

Official balls are made by all recognized manufacturers and their prices are standard. Care of the ball is important because of its cost. After proper inflation and use, balls should be stored in cool, clean rooms. They should never be kicked, sat on, or hit into rough and irregular surfaces.

TECHNIQUES
OF PARTICIPATION

INDIVIDUAL FUNDAMENTALS

There is an ever present effort in volleyball to force misplays and errors through aggressive and accurate play. With a knowledge of fundamentals a player will gain the poise and confidence that are vital to team sports. The fundamentals of volleyball listed in their order of play are as follows:

1. The serve
2. Receiving the serve—the pass
3. The set-up
4. The spike
5. The block

Every effort should be made to master *all* the fundamentals to become a well-balanced player. (Note: The description of all techniques are for right-handed players—necessary modifications should be made for left-handed players.)

THE SERVE

Regard the serve as an opportunity to score. For some reason, players seem to approach the serve from extremes. One player will simply "put the ball into play" by batting it over the net without any definite plan in mind; others will go to the opposite extreme, using a wild roundhouse serve in the hope that the sheer power of the serve itself will score a point. This latter type of serve has about a 50 per cent chance of resulting in a service fault.

The server should approach the service line with deliberation, taking sufficient time to follow through with a plan to score.

Of first importance is avoiding service faults (hitting balls into the net or out of bounds). National championship teams have calculated that 90 per cent or more of the serves must be good if the team is to win.

Second most important is the ability to serve the ball to a specific area, position, or player on the court, in order to take advantage of weaknesses in the opponent's lineup. At times, serving to a weak ball handler is effective; at other times, aiming at a position on the court to avoid setting up plays for the opposition's most powerful spiker may be the best strategy. Direct the serves to areas on the court that are known to make any possible planned attack or offensive most difficult.

The third most important point to remember is to contact the ball in a manner that will cause the receiver and his teammates the maximum amount of trouble in handling or making a pass. It is rather common to see players put the ball in play by hitting it underhand with the hand or fist, but only occasionally are such serves effective.

The Roundhouse Serve

With long, diligent practice, the roundhouse serve can be kept in the court and directed with such force as to be considered an acceptable serve. The server faces the right side of the court, his left shoulder toward the net. He tosses the ball into the air at a point slightly above and behind his right shoulder. With his hand cupped, he contacts the ball as it falls to a point about even with the top of his head. The ball, hit with great force with the heel of the hand, gains topspin as the rigid fingers pass over its top. Good form requires a smooth follow-through. The degree of arc is governed by the amount of topspin, which, in turn, is controlled by the position and force of the hit. These complications allow for greater possibility of error, and, although the roundhouse can at times be effective, a more simple serve is advised. (Many European teams use this service.)

The Overhead Serve

The overhead (tennis type) serve is one that will readily meet all of the requirements: (1) it is good over 90 per cent of the time; (2) it is easily placed accurately; (3) it furnishes the greatest problems for serve receivers. Because it meets these requirements it is the one used by most leading players. The technique of hitting this serve is as follows: (1) the server faces the net either with his feet together or with his left foot slightly forward of his right; (2) he tosses the ball carefully with both hands (so that it does not spin) about 2–3 feet above his head and about 18 inches forward; (3) he hits the ball with either the heel of his hand or a flat fist, reaching far above his head and in line with his shoulder in a manner very similar to that used in serving in tennis. (See Illustration 4.) The server makes an effort to hit the ball in such a manner that it will *not* spin. If the ball passes over the net and every seam on the ball can be seen to be holding its position and not turning, then it can be expected that the ball will float, drop, curve, or perform in a manner that will keep the opposition guessing as to just what the ball might be doing at the moment that it is received.

The Drop Serve

Some players hit the ball with just enough force to cross the net and drop quickly into the opponent's court. This serve is similar to the overhead serve except that the arm is bent and the ball is

Illustration 4

contacted at eye level, contacting lower than the other types of serves.

The Underhand Serve

The underhand serve has the same characteristics as the overhead serve except that the force, the angle of passing over the net, and the action of the ball are minimized. The underhand serve is easy to learn, but opponents seldom have difficulty receiving it. In performing this serve the player stands with his left foot advanced and pointed directly toward the net. The knees are slightly bent and the body faces the net. The left arm reaches across the body, holding the ball in the palm at arm's length and in a position so that, when the right arm is swung in a line toward the net, the right hand will strike the ball when dropped or tossed by the left hand. Contact is made with the heel of the right hand or with the fist, palms toward the net.

Common Mistakes Made in Serving

A common mistake made in hitting the underhand serve is bending the left elbow and hitting the ball underneath, making it move toward the ceiling instead of directly over the net. If the right arm is bent, the ball will be struck near the top and will not clear the net. If the hitting arm does not swing straight through toward the net, it will not contact the ball solidly and the ball may not reach the net or may go out of bounds.

A common mistake made in hitting the overhead serve is throwing the ball too far forward so that the ball is contacted at the bottom and fails to cross the net. If the ball is thrown too far back of the server, it will be hit out of bounds or toward the ceiling, depending on the force of the hit. If the hitting arm does not move straight through, the ball is sideswiped or not contacted solidly, and it will be hit out of bounds or short of the net. Too much shifting or walking while the ball is tossed will affect the swing action of the hitting arm so that solid contact with the ball is lost. It is very important to contact the back of the ball solidly and with the proper force to achieve the desired results.

There is no short cut in learning the serve and much time must be spent in practice to develop balance, proper contact, and feel. *The serve is the most effective scoring weapon in volleyball.*

RECEIVING THE SERVE—THE PASS

Serve receiving is the key to volleyball success. If the first ball passed does not come accurately up to the front line, the set-up man must chase it, and his set, being made from an awkward position, will be difficult to handle.

The spiker has a much greater chance of making an error with a poor set. As the serve passes over the net, a player cannot move toward the ball and reach the spot precisely when the ball comes down. If the ball is misjudged even slightly, or if it takes an unexpected hop or drop, the receiver will not have enough time to get into proper position. It is most important to hurry to the spot and *wait for the ball to come down,* with hands raised in the receiving position over the head, knees bent, and feet in a solid position on the floor. The left foot should be forward of the right. The thumbs and the index fingers of both hands should be about 2–3 inches apart. As the ball drops, so should the hands and knees. The wrists should be tilted backward. (See Illustration 5.) All fingers (and thumbs) contact the ball simultaneously; then, as the ball springs off the fingers, the wrists and knees are straightened. This seemingly simple skill is so important that it warrants more than half of the practice time. Some important points to remember are: consistently get into position to face the point to which the ball is directed; arch the ball, after removing all of the spin, so that it drops straight down toward the waiting set-up man. This latter fundamental is the stamp of an accomplished volleyball player.

Illustration 5

The Fist or Bounce Pass

In most of our instructions in playing the ball we have assumed the ideal situation, where the player has the opportunity and the time to get under a ball and play it properly with a chest pass. Many times during play the player will not have the time or position to meet the ball under such favorable conditions. It then becomes necessary to know what to do when, for instance, a ball has reached a point only 2–3 feet from the floor. In such cases the ball may best be played with (1) the heel of the hand (see Illustration 6), (2) a rigidly cupped hand, or (3) the closed fist.

When the fist is used, the fingers are tightly clenched with knuckles pointed downward. Knees are bent and the ball is allowed to reach a point about 12–18 inches above the floor before the fist is shoved directly under the center of the ball; contact is made directly upward. With sufficient practice, this shot can be mastered so that a dead ball, with no spin on it, can be brought up to a playable position.

The player can use his fist for "digs" on spikes that can hardly be seen as much more than a blur by dropping it under the ball and "giving" or dropping back a little as contact is made. The ball will bounce up into playable position from the force of the spike.

Illustration 6

Illustration 7

The Forearm Bounce Pass

When, as a result of a difficult serve, a ball comes in fast and low, or is hit directly toward a player at such an angle that it is impossible to bend down and use the chest pass, the forearm bounce may be used, as shown in Illustration 7. The hands are quickly clasped together, the elbows are rotated inward to align the forearms side by side, and the body crouches with the knees slightly bent. The forearms and hands are placed parallel to the floor, and contact is made squarely on the hands, wrists, or forearms. As contact is made, the knees and body are straightened slightly, with an easy motion, in order to give an upward bounce to the ball.

It is to be understood that this type of play is an emergency play and should not be used in the place of the chest pass. It should be used only when the ball is below the waist because of a hard serve, a spike, or a loose ball that drops below the waist.

THE SET-UP

The first step to combat an opponent's effort to score through his service was explained in the last section on receiving the serve. If an effective and accurate pass reaches the front line, the set-up man's job is not too difficult. Most championship teams have their front court set-up man shift to a position in the center of the court immediately after the serve is hit (unless of course, he is already in this position). As the ball comes up from the backcourt, the set-up man squarely faces one of the side lines, in a position similar to that described in receiving the serve (see Illustration 8). The ball, instead of coming down forward of the position faced, should be dropping

Illustration 8

directly on top of the set-up man's head. The palms of the hands face upward and the head is bent back. The set-up man can follow the ball through the "window" made by the position of his hands above his head. The most effective attack by spikers, in order to avoid the block, is customarily made along the net near the side lines. For that reason the set-up man can most effectively do his job if he can hold his position and not make his intention known to the opposition in advance. When the decision must finally be made, a quick step backward would be best for setting to the end position in front; a quick step forward would be best for setting to the position behind.

The ball is contacted in the same manner as it is in a pass from the backcourt. The ideal set is usually within 18 inches of the net at a height approximately 5 feet over the top of the net (see Illustration 9). It is best to have the ball drop straight down (as if dropped from above) when it reaches a point near the end of the court where the spiker is waiting. There are many variations of the set, and with teamwork and practice the set can be made considerably lower and even passed out rather quickly to one end or the other in order to avoid the blockers.

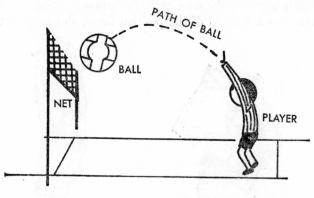

Illustration 9

All of the above is predicated on the assumption that the set-up man receives a perfect pass from the serve receiver. When the pass is not perfect, the set-up man must adjust; he must move quickly back under a ball that has been poorly passed and get in a position whenever possible to be able to make a set-up to either end. If, however, he must chase back deeper into the court, he will often have only one of the spikers to whom he can effectively make the pass. In such a case he should remember that the ball should be set up in such a manner that it will be high enough to drop as straight down as possible when it reaches its position near the net, so that the spiker may have the best angle for spiking the ball. (For the beginner it is advised that all players face directly toward the spot to which they intend to pass the ball.)

THE SPIKE IN GENERAL

The spike is the most spectacular and thrilling play in volleyball. In the earlier days of volleyball, a parallel approach along the net with a one-foot take-off was used, but it has long since been discarded because of its many disadvantages. With the advent of the three- and four-man block, so many spikes were blocked back that a spiker traveling parallel with the net was in no position to retrieve them.

Illustration 10

The straight-in approach with a two-foot take-off has taken its place almost entirely and has overcome the disadvantages of the older style.

The spiker stations himself along one of the side lines approximately 10 feet back from the net. When the ball is set up, he starts his approach. The number of steps in the approach varies widely from spiker to spiker; some spikers use only three steps, while others use more. As he reaches a position about 3 feet behind the ball, he starts his jump, concentrating on going up rather than forward. The ball drops in line with the shoulder of the arm making the hit, and contact is made with the ball when it is approximately 18 inches in front of the spiker. These distances vary somewhat according to the style of the spiker. Some spikers who use considerable wrist action often hit the ball at a point as much as a foot higher than their heads; others prefer to have the ball drop lower. As the spiker makes his jump (usually from a crouch), both arms swing vigorously upward; then, as contact is made with the ball, the wrist is snapped, most of the force coming from the heel of the hand. See Illustration 10 for a spiking sequence. This snap imparts a hard downward thrust and the use of the heel of the hand allows a sharp downward angle. There are spikers who spike the ball effectively with their hand cupped, thus allowing the ball to be contacted at a height 2–3 inches higher than usual. (Hitting the ball with the fingers will usually cause the ball to be thrown, which is illegal.)

The spike described above is the orthodox kill, which is executed from the position most desired and under conditions most ideal.

The Topspin Spike

When it becomes necessary to hit a ball from a position considerably further back from the net, because the pass or the set lacks

the desired accuracy, the approach can be made in a similar manner, but the ball is contacted slightly *behind* the head, with the heel of the hand or with the hand cupped. As the ball is hit, a follow-through motion with rigid fingers, seemingly with an effort to wrap the hand around the top of the ball, will result in a topspin, which will give the ball an arc that will cause it to curve down sharply. If the ball is hit with enough topspin, it will land on the opponent's court rather than out of bounds. With practice, players can learn to spike effectively from 5 or 10 feet back of the net. (See Illustration 11.)

Illustration 11

It should be noted that the spiker should position himself in such a manner that he will be making his approach as straight into the net as possible. If the set-up is slightly off to the left or the right the correction should be made by the spiker *before* he starts his take-off, so that he will be running in the proper direction toward the net. (See Illustration 12.)

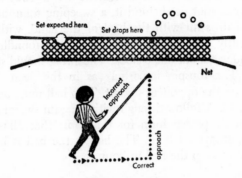

Illustration 12

This direct net approach will allow a spiker (1) to drive a ball straight down, (2) to drive to the right side of the court by moving slightly to the left, and (3) to drive sharply to the left side of the court by a simple turn of the shoulder. His approach and take-off will not indicate to the opposition which of these shots he intends to use.

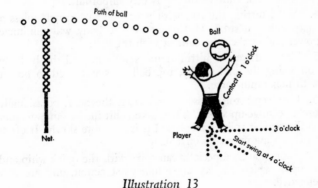

Illustration 13

The Roundhouse Spike

There is one more basic spike that should be mastered—the round-house. This spike should be used when a spiker must hit a ball from a position back from the net and when he is unable to get into a position to attack the ball in the orthodox manner (with the ball between himself and the net). When the ball is away from the net and the spiker cannot get behind it, a sweeping roundhouse motion is used. The ball is hit with the heel of the hand, with the fingers and palm tightly cupped (as they are for the roundhouse serve). The hit is made at about one o'clock. The swing should start at about four o'clock. The topspin imparted (as in the deep set kill) will keep the ball on the opponent's court. This ball must be *hit hard* to avoid being held. A follow-through with the arm swinging across the face will promote proper form for this shot. (See Illustration 13.) Never let up; always hit hard. The harder the ball is hit, the more spin imparted to keep the ball in bounds.

Learning to Spike

1. Learn to jump *up* instead of forward.

2. Try to jump high and hit the ball hard. Coordinating jumping and hitting is difficult because the ball is in the hitting zone above the net for only a fraction of a second.

3. Approach the net as the ball is on the way up from the set; jump as the ball begins to descend. If you jump as the ball goes up, your descent may precede that of the ball, and you may miss. Correct timing is very important.

4. Avoid hitting the ball with your side to the net unless a sharp cut is desired. Hitting across the body will minimize power and weaken the contact with the ball.

5. Try to drive the hitting hand solidly behind the ball. By contacting the ball solidly, the ball does not need to be hit with maximum force.

6. On deep set-up passes (away from the net), occasionally use a "change-up spike." This spike is hit in the same manner as the regular spike, except that it is hit more slowly. It often catches the opponents off balance.

7. Short players especially can spike with the quick whip and topspin, which employ maximum wrist action, and are very effective.

THE BLOCK

The block is the attempt to intercept the ball at the net rather than allowing backcourt players to take their chances on trying to retrieve hard-driven spikes. Because an effectively spiked ball can, and often does, travel in excess of 100 miles per hour, it is necessary to form a strong block at the net in order to stop powerful spikers. Professor McCloy of the State University of Iowa clocked a spiked volleyball at speeds in excess of 117 miles per hour—faster than any other hand-propelled ball in any sport. There is no limitation on the number of players that can block, but championship teams usually use three or four men. Customarily the three forecourt men are used with one of the backcourt men, usually selected for his blocking skill. The men are deployed about evenly across the front of the court as soon as the service is made, the backcourt man moving quickly into a forward position to which he has previously been assigned. The blockers watch the ball from their positions approximately 4 feet back from the net, until the play has definitely developed beyond recall. All four of these men try to reach a position at which they can form a solid screen of hands across the top of the net to block the spike from the opposing team. (See Illustration 14.)

The blocking player must be alert so that he may quickly move into position, where he can place his hands above the top of the net with thumbs touching, heels of the hands pushed forward, and fingers

Illustration 14

bent slightly back. He has reached his position when he can feel his shoulder lightly contact his blocking teammate next to him. This position should be about 2 feet back from the net. He jumps slightly *after* the spiker has jumped. Blocking requires real teamwork. The key man in a block is usually the outside blocker, or end man. He takes the extreme outside position and the other men quickly move into position, shoulder to shoulder, to form a solid wall beside him. In actual practice, good teams are usually satisfied if they can get three blockers into the play. In such a case, the fourth blocker drops back into a position on the court where he can retrieve a ball off the block, or return a spike that may be angled around the block.

There are two types of blocks: (1) the hard block, in which the hands are kept rigid in an attempt to force the ball back to the court of the spiker, and (2) the soft block, in which the hands roll back in an effort to retrieve the ball on one's own side of the court. This latter blocking is customarily used by better fielding teams.

When the front line includes a very short man, it may be well to shift two men to the front line to block, and shift the shorter man to the backcourt to cover. If he was the set-up man, one of the backcourt men must clearly be assigned as temporary set-up man.

BASIC OFFENSIVE PATTERNS

A team is on the offensive when it controls the ball. Therefore, all players must make an effort to be in the right place and position in order to control the ball completely when it is on their side of the net.

When receiving the serve, players should be positioned in such a manner that a good pass will result. The formation for their positions is basically crescent shaped, regardless of how it may be varied. No player should stand in front of or block the view of another player. Since it is virtually impossible for the opponents to serve the ball into the front 4 or 5 feet of the court, the crescent formation starts about 15 feet back from the net. Illustration 15 shows the crescent formation in receiving the serve. The rules state that every man must clearly be in his rotation order, with all frontcourt men forward of all backcourt men; no overlapping is allowed.

The system most popularly used in this country is the 4–2 (four spikers and two set-up men). Let us assume for the moment that the front line set-up man is in the center front position in the rotation order and the service is coming from the left side of the court (the serving team's right side); an effective receiving formation would place the players in positions shown in Illustration 15.

Note that the spiker in the left front position is almost standing on the left side line. A serve coming straight down the line travels a short distance, and the left front player can move forward easily to cover balls that may be served just over the net on his side; however, he does not drop back more than a step or two on deep serves, which are the responsibility of the left back player, who must also cover short serves not more than a step or so in front of him as well as all serves behind the left front man and those behind the center back man.

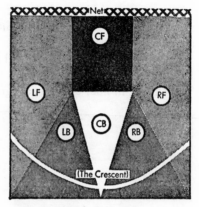

Illustration 15

The right back man has essentially the same assignment on the right side of the court.

The center front player, a set-up man, stays close to the net, out of the play if possible, and watches for serves that are but a short distance back or to the left or right. Such serves are usually soft and easy to handle, so he is ever alert either (1) to set this first ball up directly to a spiker or (2) to pass the ball straight up high so that the other setter (center back) may move into position to make the set.

The right front spiker can position himself about 4 feet from the side line, because the serve made from the left side does not come down his side line, but travels diagonally, giving him more time to move toward the side line and deeper into the court because of the longer distance the ball has to travel.

A serve coming straight down the center would allow symmetrical receiving formations with left front and right front about 3 feet in from the side lines, and the others in their usual positions.

We are faced with a little different situation when the set-up man is in the left front or right front position in the rotation order. This position presents a greater challenge to proper serve receiving, as the setter (left front) now must stay as close to the side line as possible to allow the spiker (center front) also to be positioned as close to the side line as he can. This arrangement allows the spiker to receive any serves that come straight down the line. While the rotation rules confine the setter to the left forward position and the spiker to a position to his right, the moment the ball is hit by the server the setter moves quickly to the center and the spiker moves to the left side line so that they end up in the same relative positions that they are in on Illustration 15.

Because the ball needs to travel as little as 30 feet from the server to the net, there is still not time to be positioned exactly as before. The change in floor coverage assignments is shown in Illustration 16.

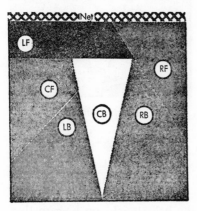
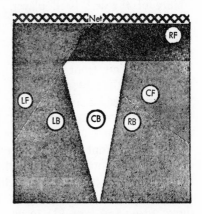

Illustration 16   *Illustration 17*

Again remember Illustration 16 is for floor assignments for the serve coming down the left side line; right side line serves would reverse assignments (for center front and right front only).

When the set-up man is in the right front position, essentially the same situation prevails (see Illustration 17).

When a team is receiving the serve, teammates should back up the receiver in an effort to keep the play alive in case of a misplay. At least one player should run behind him; another player should be alert to cover in front. All others should face him in case the ball is deflected in their direction.

Confusion about assignments in serve receiving can cost a team more points than any other mistake in volleyball. The individual skill of handling the ball properly is paramount, but teamwork is necessary for the success of the key play in volleyball—the first ball pass from the backcourt.

Covering the Spike

Now the ball has been passed up from the backcourt, the set-up has been made toward one of the side lines, and the spiker is about to kill the ball. The temptation to admire the play and to become a spectator has to be overcome, for the opposition has put its blocking machinery into motion—a split second after the ball is spiked, it may crash back onto the spiker's court with the same speed. It is the rule, rather than the exception, that the ball usually must be spiked several times before a point (or side-out) is won.

It is difficult to determine exactly each player's position because of the possibility of the spiker using different speeds or directions for his kill.

It is best to be alert for any action and variations that may develop. A crouched position, with hands up about shoulder high and feet apart, ready to move quickly in any direction, is most effective. Facing the action while studying all possible moves, changes, and habits of teammates and opposing players may give the key to the action to come. This perception is one difference between the ordinary and the best players.

The best position for covering a spike on the right-hand side of the court is shown in Illustration 18.

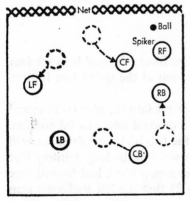

Illustration 18

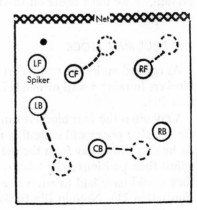

Illustration 19

Note that the spiker (right front) is backed up very closely by the right back man who, crouched low with hands high, is ready for a ball blocked sharply downward. The set-up man, after making his set from a closer net position, has moved away from the net to take blocked balls angled sharply downward toward the center of the court. The left forward man watches for longer laterals. The center back man must cover the deep balls blocked over the heads of the center front and right back men. The left back man "floats" around very deep in the backcourt. Because he is furthest from the ball, and because he is more likely to receive a high ball, he is often the key man in re-starting the offensive play. A good defensive team, expecting the ball to be blocked, will usually maintain control, passing the ball recovered from the block up to the set-up man, who then sets it out to either end for another spike.

Sets on the left side of the net reverse these assignments (see Illustration 19).

BASIC DEFENSIVE PATTERNS

The moment a team is on the defensive, the big effort is directed toward gaining control of the ball.

The quickest and most ideal defense is to block a hard spike back down into the opponent's court. Blocking methods and patterns were covered previously, so we will not spend further time discussing them here. However, the somewhat less than ideal defensive situation often prevails, so we must figure on the best methods to cover unexpected developments.

THE FOUR-MAN BLOCK

As covered under the section on The Block, the goal is to get four blockers forming a wall of hands in front of the spiker (see Illustration 20).

Very often the four blockers cannot get into the play on time and a good, alert player will sense this and drop off into a useful position. As he does drop away from the net, the two backcourt defenders will adjust their positions as he takes over some of the large territory that they would have had to cover if a four-man block had formed (see Illustration 21). Note in Illustration 21 that the left backcourt man

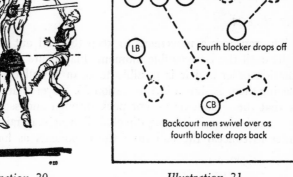

Fourth blocker drops off

Backcourt men swivel over as
fourth blocker drops back

Illustration 20   Illustration 21

is responsible for the drop (or "dink") shots which a spiker may place over the heads of the blockers while they are in the air.

If the play develops to the right side and the blockers shift to the right side of the net, the "wing" (right backcourt man) will drop close behind the blockers to eliminate the effectiveness and threat of this shot. The backcourt space left open when the wing man moves close to the net must be covered by the center back. If the blockers fail to close a gap and the spike comes through a hole, a good court

Illustration 22   Illustration 23

man will see it coming and will be ready for it. The most effective stance is to be ready to move quickly in all directions. Note the position of players in Illustration 22.

THE SCREEN

The screen is a movement to keep the ball out of the receiver's sight until the last possible moment. Players are required to stay in rotation order and it is possible to form a wall of five players by placing them as shown in Illustration 23. Players stand close together so that the opponents cannot peek through and see when the ball is hit and where it is being directed. Players may raise their arms in order to conceal the ball from the opponents as long as possible.

RULES

THE GAME

Volleyball is played by two teams of six players each whose primary objective is to make the ball hit the floor on the opponent's side of the net. Conversely, in order to win they must keep the ball from hitting the floor on their own side of the net. Only the team serving can score points; if the serving team fails to return the ball properly, it loses the right to serve to the other team. No point is scored for either team; the serve merely exchanges sides. When this occurs the receiving team players must rotate clockwise one position. Thus, the player in the left back position moves to the left front position, the player in left front moves to center front, and so on, around the court.

The first play of the game is the serve, which is made by the right back player. He stands behind the end line, anywhere between the side lines. His first attempt must be good because no "let" serve (a serve that may be replayed because it has hit the net) is allowed. The receiving team may play the ball no more than three times before it goes back over the net. The ball must be played in the air and must be clearly hit or battered; it may not be thrown or lifted.

GENERAL RULES

1. Captains toss a coin for choice of serve and court.
2. The first server is the right back player and he may not touch the boundary line while hitting the serve. He may strike the ball with his hand in any manner—underhand, sidearm, or overhand.
3. In playing the ball, all players must clearly hit or bat the ball.
4. No player may encroach on the opponent's court. The center line, under the net, may be stepped on but not over.

5. No player may reach over or contact the net.

6. No player may play the ball twice in succession *unless* two players touch the ball simultaneously as in passing or blocking the ball. A player may play the ball on the first and third hit.

7. Each team may not play the ball more than three times before it is returned over the net.

8. If a ball touches the boundary line it is good.

9. A player may run outside his own court to play a ball.

10. The ball, to be legal, must pass between or over the side boundary lines as it crosses the net.

11. A team wins the game when that team scores fifteen points and has a two-point advantage, or if, at the termination of the 8 minutes' ball-in-play time, that team has a two-point advantage.

12. A match consists of the best two out of three games.

13. The team that did not serve the first game will serve the second game.

14. The teams exchange courts at the end of each game.

15. After the serve, players may take any position on their side of the court.

16. Two time-outs are allowed each team during each game.

17. A player may re-enter the game twice but only to his original position. (In women's games, a player may enter twice.) Starting the game counts as an entry.

18. Any or all players are allowed to block at the net.

19. Any front-line player may spike the ball at the net. Back-line players may spike at the net providing they land with both feet on or behind a line 7½ feet from the net. (In women's games, if a back-line player comes up to "save the ball" and does not interfere with another player, or is not playing it because of a weak player in that position, the official will not call a foul. However, if a back-line player comes up to spike the ball, a foul should be called.)

SPECIFIC RULES *

Court (Rule 2.00)

The dimensions of the volleyball court, including net dimensions, are shown in Illustration 1, in the chapter on Equipment (Chapter 3).

---

* For complete official rules, consult *Official Volleyball Rule Book and Guide*, Berne, Indiana: Published annually by the United States Volleyball Association.

Server and Player Positions (Rule 4.00–6.00)

The server is the right back player of the serving team. His position must be anywhere behind the end line and within the side lines. Other players must be in rotation order before the ball is struck on the service. After the ball is struck on the serve, players may interchange positions anywhere on the court. (In women's games, however, a foul may be called if a player persistently interchanges positions during play.) In an official game, a team consists of six players.

Choice of Sides or Service (Rule 5.00–7.00)

1. *For the first game,* the winner of the toss has the choice of serving or receiving, or the choice of courts.
2. *In subsequent games,* teams shall change courts at the end of each game of the same match, and shall alternate the beginning serve.
3. *In the middle of the third game,* teams shall automatically change courts after one team has scored eight points; or first time the ball becomes dead after 4 minutes of ball in play in an official time game.

Serving Faults (Rule 13.00–14.00)

The service is a fault if the server:
1. Does not take the proper position before serving.
2. Commits a foot fault.
3. Hits the ball into the net—no "let" serves are allowed.
4. Hits the ball so it crosses outside the side lines as it passes over the net.
5. Hits the ball into any post or overhead structure, unless special ground rules are followed.

A Side-Out for Serving Team (Rule 13.00–14.00)

The serving team loses the ball for service when:
1. Any service fault occurs.
2. Any member of the serving team is not in proper rotation order.
3. Any serving team player reaches over or contacts the net.
4. The serving team fails to return the ball over the net with a minimum of three hits, or illegally plays the ball.
5. The serving team players use directing remarks, stomp their feet, or wave their hands to distract an opponent.

6. Serving team players step *over* the center line (they may step on this line, however).
7. There is an illegal substitution.
8. Excess time-outs occur.
9. The server serves out of turn.
10. A back-line player spikes the ball within 7½ feet of the net.

A *Point for the Serving Team* (Rule 13.00–14.00)

A point is scored when:
1. Opponents fail to return the ball legally within a minimum of three hits.
2. Opponents illegally play the ball.
3. Opponents contact the net, reach over the net, or step over the center line.
4. Opponents use excess time-out.
5. Illegal substitution occurs by opponent.
6. Opponents are not in proper rotation order as the ball is served.
7. Opponents are guilty of unsportsmanlike conduct.

Substitution (Rule 11.00)

1. A substitution may be made only when the ball is dead.
2. The substitute should report to the scorer first, then to the umpire (in women's games, to the referee).
3. A substitute must be ready for play when he reports and may not take a warm-up period.
4. A substitute shall take the position of the player whom he is replacing and if he re-enters later must substitute for the same player regardless of his position on the court.
5. A substitute may not enter a game more than twice. (See page 34, rule 17.)

Scoring (Rule 18.00)

A game is won by either team when:
1. One team scores fifteen points first with a two-point advantage.
2. In an official game, a team scores fifteen points with a two-point advantage before time expires; or at the end of 8 minutes playing time, when one team has a two-point advantage.
3. For any reason a team is reduced to less than six players (the

game shall be forfeited). The score of a forfeited game is 15–0 (in women's games, 1–0).

A match is won by the team that wins two games out of three.

*Officials (Rule 3.00)**

Referee's position is at one end of and above the net. His responsibilities are to:

1. Decide when the ball is in play.
2. Decide when the ball is dead.
3. Decide when a point is made.
4. Decide when a side is out.
5. Overrule decisions of the other officials.
6. Direct a replay of any service.
7. Make decisions not covered in the rules.

Umpire has a position opposite the referee and stands beneath the top of the net. His responsibilities are to:

1. Assist the referee in calling violations, fouls, and players out of position.
2. Authorize substitutions.
3. Call violations on the center line.
4. Keep official time of time-outs, injuries, and time between games.

Scorer has a position opposite the referee. His responsibilities are to:

1. Handle all scoring devices.
2. Record names of players, their numbers, and playing order.
3. Notify referee of incorrect positions or service when ball is dead. Either captain may request a check on opponent's line-up.
4. Record the score, time-outs, and substitutions.

Linesmen have positions outside and near the corners of the court. They call foot faults on the server and signal when the ball lands near the side or end line, whether the ball was in or out of court. They hold the ball when time is out.

* For officials in women's games, see Rule 6 in *Volleyball Guide* (July 1963-July 1965), Division for Girls and Women's Sports, American Association for Health, Physical Education, and Recreation, Washington, D.C.

Time Factors (*Rule 10.00*)

The following time factors are in effect:

1. The rest period between games of a match is 3 minutes.
2. Time-out shall not exceed 1 minute.
3. Two time-outs are allowed each team per game and may not be taken consecutively.
4. Time for injury shall not exceed 3 minutes (for women, 5 minutes.)

Playing the Ball (*Rule 9.00*)

The following rules apply when playing the ball:

1. The ball must be clearly hit (not caught or held).
2. Simultaneous contacts of teammates are considered one play.
3. One player may not make successive contacts of the ball except from a hard spike if it constitutes one attempt to play the ball. (In women's games, if two or more players from opposing teams contact the ball simultaneously above the net, this simultaneous contact shall not be considered as one of the three contacts allowed a team. The players involved are eligible to participate in the next play which shall be considered the first of three contacts allowed to the team.)
4. A player may go outside his court to play the ball, if he does not cross the center line or its assumed extension.
5. If two opposing players contact the ball simultaneously directly above the net, either may play the ball on the next hit.
6. The ball is dead if it crosses the net outside the side line, touches the ceiling or posts holding the net, or lands out of bounds.
7. If a spike strikes a multiple block, it is considered one play and any player making the block may next play the ball.

TRAINING PROGRAM

Volleyball Requires Peak Conditioning

All athletes should strive for the best possible physical condition before they perform. It is important, however, that players consider more than just physical condition; a good volleyball player should have not only strength, endurance, agility, and coordination, but also a strong competitive instinct, the ability to relax, and sound social, mental, and emotional stability. Volleyball players should strive for the following objectives:

1. To develop strength, endurance, and speed.
2. To develop neuromuscular skills and agility.
3. To develop honesty and fair play.
4. To develop good sportsmanship and emotional control.
5. To develop social adjustment.
6. To develop wholesome recreation with team play and group cooperation.

The champion develops himself completely in all phases of these requirements and objectives through conscious (and sometimes subconscious) evaluation of his performance in comparison with these high standards. The champion is not satisfied with mediocrity when it applies to his specialty.

Physical Training

An athlete must work hard to develop strength, endurance, agility, and speed. A good series of exercises designed to develop these traits in volleyball are as follows:
1. Rub the hands with fingers interlaced and clap the hands together. Alternate these exercises for 1 minute.
2. While holding arms out from the sides (parallel to floor) rotate them in small and large circles forward and backward for 2 minutes.

3. Stretching exercises—bend sideways, forward, and rotate in circles from the waist. Toe-touching may be substituted.

4. Do at least twenty-five push-ups.

5. Explosive jump—on count one, jump upward, swinging arms waist high. On count two, land on floor, arms swinging downward and backward. On count three, from a crouch position jump vigorously and swing arms vigorously upward as high as possible. On count four, land on floor ready to resume count one.

6. Do at least twenty-five sit-ups.

7. Run at least 1 mile a day just before and during the early competitive season.

The training program should be a daily affair for best results. In view of the frequency of injuries to the feet and hands in volleyball, daily performance of these exercises is necessary to strengthen and prepare these body parts to withstand the severe demands made on them during competition.

Participation in other physical activity and team sports is especially encouraged because it will teach qualities of alertness, agility, and teamwork, which are vitally important in team sports.

In any training program, it is understood that the body has certain needs. It undergoes changes according to the extent of the player's present participation and physical background. The athlete who is presently in top physical condition and who has had past experience in playing volleyball will not experience as much discomfort as a result of the first day of drills as will a person who has not participated at all or who is not in good condition. Strenuous physical activity may cause such things as excess perspiration, muscle soreness, weight reduction, and extreme fatigue. However, as the training program progresses, the body adapts itself to the rigorous demands placed upon it, and the undesirable symptoms disappear or at least are greatly diminished.

As in all walks of life there will be those who are shirkers—players who will not follow instructions and who will not maintain training rules. If exercises are to be given each day it has been found beneficial to have everyone in class or on the team take his turn at leading the group. This tends to stimulate all to work harder and then, if necessary, a few words to the lazy ones usually help to bring them into the full program.

Mental Training

An athlete must be taught to work hard to develop strong mental attitudes toward honesty and fair play. Most players want to win and seem to enjoy the activity more when they win. Unfortunately, some players become obstinate, grouchy, and quick to give excuses when they lose. Winning and losing must be taken in stride.

A good athlete plays fair and, furthermore, is honest in his thinking about the game. He realizes that he must know how to execute every fundamental, when to execute it, and what to expect his opponent to do. This realization develops poise and confidence that could be interpreted as morale. A keen desire to excel and to win, along with high morale and the better performance that comes from more experience, are the makings of a champion.

Team spirit is nothing more than the confidence each player has in himself and his teammates and the belief that his team can defeat the opponent. This team spirit (or morale) is based upon the knowledge of fundamentals, a desire to compete and to win, courage, pride, and, finally, an honest love for the game.

A training program is not complete unless it includes proper mental attitudes of the player toward the game, toward himself, toward his opponents, and toward spectators.

Emotional Training

The athlete is expected to control his emotions. Emotional control is probably the hardest problem an athlete encounters, especially when he is being defeated by a supposedly inferior team. There is no set rule that an athlete must smile when he wins or loses. There is no set rule that he must not grumble or complain to teammates. The coach sets rules and regulations of team conduct. He no doubt will insist that there is someone who can beat you—maybe not today but tomorrow. The coach will tell and show every possible way for a play to be made and how it is to be defended. A smart athlete will recognize the play and will try to defend it the way he knows best. If the opponent wins, the loser can only admit that the opponent took advantage of his mistakes and weaknesses and played better. If a loser complains, the coach should include an emphasis on emotional control in his training program.

Social Adjustment

Finally, an athlete must adjust socially in order to participate wholeheartedly in activities. It is true that some players thrive on praise and kindness and will give their all when encouraged by the coach. On the other hand, other players may need to be bullied, scolded, and threatened in order to play all out. The crux of the matter is that each player is an individual and will function best under his own individually prescribed treatment. Generally speaking, praise is a better motivator than ridicule, and should be used lavishly.

GLOSSARY

7

Ace: A point scored as the direct result of the serve.

Attack: Play in which the spike or kill is used.

Ball in play: The ball is in play from the time it is served until it becomes a dead ball.

Back-line spiker: A back-line offensive player who spikes the ball on or behind a line 7½ feet from the net. (In women's games, a back-line spiker would be illegal.)

Block: Defensive play by one or more players who attempt to intercept a ball at the point where it crosses the net.

Bye: Usually given to a seeded team in a tournament when there are more or less than eight, sixteen, or thirty-two teams entered so that that team may play in later rounds.

Change of pace: A spiked or served ball hit at other than usual speed.

Cover: To be responsible for a certain area of the court; also, to back up a teammate.

Cross-court pass: A long pass from one side of the court to the other.

Dead ball: A ball not in play, after a point is scored or a side-out is declared.

Defense: A team is on defense whenever the ball is alive and controlled by the opponents.

Defensive player: Any player on a team that does not have control or possession of the ball.

Delayed spike: A ball spiked as the player descends from his jump.

Dig (or Save): Recovery of a hard-driven spike or other offensive shot when point (or side-out) would appear imminent.

Double foul: The act of two or more players on opposing teams committing a foul simultaneously.

Double hit: The act of a player who hits the ball twice in succession; this act counts as a foul.

Error: Misplay that may result in a point for the opponent, or a side-out.

Equilibrium: Balance and control of body movements.

Fake spike: Going through the motions of spiking, but changing to another type of shot, such as a tip.

Fake: A deceptive movement by a player to confuse the opponent (as in setting up a ball).

Follow-through: Movement of the arms, hands, or body after playing the ball.

Foot fault: Stepping into court before hitting the ball while serving or stepping out of the serving area beyond the side line extension. (In women's games, a foot fault occurs if the server steps *on* or over the end line during the act of serving.)

Formation: Arrangement of players on the court, either offensive or defensive.

Foul: Rule infraction.

Held ball: A ball that comes to rest momentarily in the hand, hands, or any other part of the body. The ball must be clearly batted.

Kill: (See *Spike.*)

Linesman: An official stationed at the corner of the court to determine whether a ball touches inside the court or out. (A ball touching a line is "good.")

Live ball: A ball in play. A ball remains live from the serve until it becomes a dead ball.

Match: An official match consists of the best two out of three games.

Misplay: Failure to play ball properly, because of holding, throwing, multiple contact, etc.

Multiple block: Two or more players attempting to intercept a ball at the net.

Offense: A team is on offense when it controls the ball.

Overhead pass: A ball played on the fingertips of both hands (contact usually made over the head or in front of the face) and passed opposite the direction faced.

Out of bounds: Outside the boundary lines or tape markers.

Point: A unit of scoring.

Position: Area in court occupied by a player. When a ball is served each player must be in his respective position in rotation order (left front, center front, right front, left back, center back, or right back).

Quick spike: A spiked ball hit quickly as or before the spiker reaches the height of his jump.

Receiver: The first player to receive a ball played over the net by an opponent, usually from the serve.

Referee: Superior official of the game. He is stationed at one end of and above the net.

Rotation: Clockwise movement of players when their team receives the ball for service.

Scooping: Illegal maneuver of holding or catching the ball; usually an underhand shot.

Scorer: The official who keeps the official line-up and score.

Screen: Players standing in a position to obstruct opponents' view of the serve and server.

Service: Places ball in play. An attempt to hit the ball with the hand or arm over the net, into the opponents' court. (In women's games, the ball *must* be hit with the hand and / or forearm only.)

Service area: The area behind the back line and within the extended side lines.

Set-up: A pass made especially for position and to the best advantage for a player about to spike.

Set passer: Player who usually makes the set pass. The second passer of the attack.

Side-out: Failure to score and loss of the right to serve.

Spike: To hit the ball downward, with great force, into the opponents' court.

Spiked ball: A ball (other than a served ball) hit with force from above the net.

Spiker: A player who spikes the ball.

Sticky: A held ball or a ball that has come to rest in the hands.

Switch: Movement of players to more advantageous positions, usually done as the serve goes over the net (such as switching of set-up man to center front position). (In women's games, deliberate and persistent switching is considered illegal.)

Tape marker: Vertical marker on the net directly over boundary lines to designate the sides of the court.

Throw: Illegally playing the ball by holding or changing the direction of the ball on the hit; a ball not cleanly hit.

Tip (or Tap): A hit made to uncovered areas, usually just over the hands of the blockers.

Umpire: Official on the opposite side of the court from the referee and stationed on the floor. He assists in calling fouls, errors, and violations.

Violation: Illegal action of a team before or during the game which may result in loss of points, side-out, or loss of the game.

Volley: Continuous action in a game until the ball is dead.

SELF-TESTING
AND EVALUATION

One of the first fundamentals every volleyball player should learn is how to pass the ball. Passing is the easiest fundamental to master if the player will not "fight" the ball in performing this task, especially when a testing program is in effect. Instead of relaxing and getting the most from the muscles in passing the ball, most players rush tensely into the ball and do not perform accurately or efficiently. With a thorough knowledge of the fundamentals, and confidence in one's ability, a player need not fear a testing program.

THE VOLLEY TEST

To test the volley, or pass, a line is drawn on the floor 6 feet from and parallel to the wall. Another line is drawn on the wall 10 feet high and parallel to the floor. A player stands behind the 6-foot line, serves the ball over the 10-foot line, and continues to pass the ball

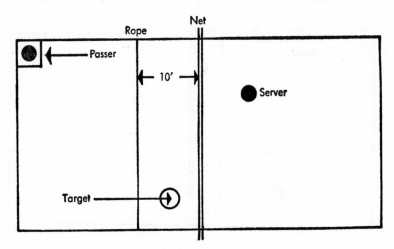

Illustration 24

back and forth above this line. In case of a miss, the ball must be served again and the count resumed with the pass. Sixty seconds are allowed for each player to volley. A stop watch is kept by someone who also counts the number of hits. The better player will have the higher number of hits and is graded accordingly.

Another test to use for passing is to stretch a rope across the court 10 feet back from the net and 12 feet high. Between the rope and the net and to one side of the court a circle 4 feet in diameter is drawn on the floor. In place of the circle a small mat or newspaper may be used, if it is of comparable size (see Illustration 24). One player is placed in the opponent's court to serve or throw the ball into the left back area, where each player in turn attempts to pass the ball over the rope and into the target area. Ten attempts are allowed and one point is given for each successful pass.

THE SET-UP TEST

To test the set-up, a rope is stretched across the court 5 feet from the net and 12 feet high (see Illustration 25). A circle 3 feet in diameter is drawn on the floor between the rope and the net at one side of the court. A player stands in the back corner of the court and tosses the ball to each player, who attempts to pass the ball over

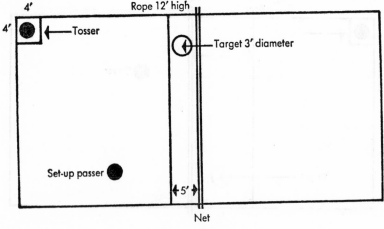

Illustration 25

the rope and into the circle. Ten attempts are given and one point is scored for each successful attempt.

THE SERVICE TEST

To test the service, a line is drawn across the court 5 feet from and parallel to the end line. The value of this area is five points. Another line is drawn on the right side (as the server faces the court) 5 feet from and parallel to the side line. The value of this area is three points. Another line is drawn on the left side 5 feet from and parallel to the side line. The value of this area is four points. The remainder of the opponent's court is given a value of two points (see Illustration 26). Each player is given ten serves (any method) and the player scoring the highest number of points is given the best grade.

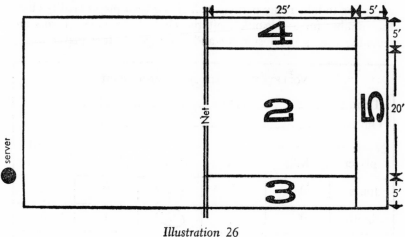

Illustration 26

THE SPIKING TEST

At the present time there is no objective test for spiking skills. However, the instructor or one of the players may toss the ball for everyone in order to have uniformity, and each player may be rated subjectively as to approach, jump, and hit. The approach should be smooth and straight toward the net. The jump should be vertical and high; the ball should be kept in front of the body. The hit should be out or downward, with force and proper hand action.

SUBJECTIVE RATINGS

In addition to the objective testing program of the serve and pass, there may be subjective rating of performance. The instructor may grade individual performance on an A, B, C, D, and F basis at the same time that the objective tests are being taken. The standards that could be used in this subjective grade are as follows: (1) how the serve or pass was controlled and how the ball reacted after contact; (2) whether the pass was high enough; (3) whether there was a violation of the rules; and (4) what the performer's attitude was toward the game as evidenced during each day's play.

During a game a scorekeeper can keep a record of performance as it affects the score. He lists a side-out kill with 0 (zero) and point kill with a 1. Ace serves are recorded with a 1. Blocks are recorded according to how many participated, giving each player credit—circle the number for a side-out; omit the circle for a point. Errors are recorded with a 0 for side-out and 1 for point. If a player had a

VOLLEYBALL SCORE SHEET AND CHART					
Team _____ vs._____ Date _____					
Officials _____ _____ Place _____					
Name of player	Kills	Aces	Blocks	Errors	Total Points
Jones	0, 1	1	②	0	2
Smith	0		②	1	0
Totals					

reasonable chance to play the ball and missed it, an error is recorded. Only the result of a point or side-out is recorded. This record will show the result of points and errors for each man.

KNOWLEDGE TEST

The following is a simple test on all phases of the game; answers will be found in the text.

TRUE-FALSE SECTION: Mark + for true, 0 for false.

_____ 1. In case of a tie score at 14–14, teams must play 3 more minutes.

_____ 2. The length of a volleyball game is 20 minutes.

_____ 3. A ball is out of bounds if it touches the post holding the net.

_____ 4. "Side-out" indicates that the serving team has just lost the serve.

_____ 5. It is a foul if a player reaches over the net.

_____ 6. In playing the ball, a player may use any part of his body.

_____ 7. In rotating, the back line players always move to their right.

_____ 8. If a ball strikes the ceiling it is called a dead ball.

_____ 9. A passed ball, other than the third pass, that strikes the net is a dead ball.

_____10. The server may stand any place behind the back line while serving.

_____11. If a player is injured his team is allowed 3 minutes before resuming the game.

_____12. A substitute may enter while the ball is being served.

_____13. A substitute doesn't have to take the position of the player whom he is replacing.

_____14. The server may step on but not over the service line while in the act of serving.

_____15. A player warming up during a time-out must spike into his own court.

_____16. A player may go outside the court to play the ball.

_____17. It is a foul to have the foot in the air over or beyond the service line on the serve.

_____18. A back line player may enter the front line area to set up the ball.

_____19. Successive contacts of the ball may be made by a defensive player on a hard spike.

_____20. Volleyball was invented in 1895.

_____21. The most popular offensive formation in competitive play is four spikers and two set-up men.

_____22. If four men block a ball, any of the four may legally play the ball for recovery after the block.

_____23. A player leaving the court during a time-out without the referee's permission is committing a violation.

_____24. If a substitute is not ready to play when a request for a substitution is made, his team shall be charged with a time-out.

_____25. A team line-up may not be changed for the match after it is once turned in to the scorer.

_____26. Points made by a player serving out of turn count if the error is not discovered before the opponent's serve.

_____27. Players may switch positions in the line-up during a game if the referee and scorekeeper are notified.

_____28. In screening, players may overlap their feet but must not overlap each other with their bodies.

_____29. A ball touched simultaneously by two players constitutes one hit.

MULTIPLE CHOICE: Place the number of the correct answer in the space provided.

_____ 1. The original name of the game was: (1) volleyball (2) bounceball   (3) handball   (4) mintonette

_____ 2. The outside dimensions of the court are: (1) 25′ x 50′ (2) 40′ x 80′   (3) 30′ x 60′   (4) 30′ x 50′   (5) 30′ x 80′

_____ 3. In the third game of a match, teams automatically change courts when either team scores: (1) 4 points   (2) 6 points (3) 8 points   (4) 10 points

_____ 4. Volleyball was invented by: (1) James Naismith   (2) George Fisher (3) A. P. Idell   (4) William Morgan (5) Howard Danford

___ 5. A player may enter the game: (1) 3 times (2) 1 time (3) 2 times (4) 4 times

___ 6. A ball touched simultaneously by two players: (1) is a foul (2) is a violation (3) constitutes one hit (4) constitutes two hits (5) can be played next by neither player

___ 7. The score of a forfeited game is: (1) 1–0 (2) 11–0 (3) 15–0 (4) 2–0 (5) 0–0

___ 8. The height of the net for college men and open play is: (1) 7'6" (2) 7'4¼" (3) 8' (4) 8'2" (5) 8'3"

___ 9. Team A is serving. A player on team B returns the ball but falls into the net after the ball touches the floor in team A's court. The score, which was 10–2, becomes: (1) 11–2 (2) 11–3 (3) 10–3 (4) 3–10 (5) 2–10

___10. Team B is serving. Team A returns the ball but a member of team B touches the net. The score which was 3–2 becomes: (1) 2–3 (2) 3–3 team A serves (3) 3–3 team B serves (4) 3–2 team A serves (5) 4–2

COMPLETION: Fill in the correct answer in the space provided.

1. A team is allowed _____ minutes between games.
2. A player may re-enter the game _____ times.
3. A team is permitted to call time out _____ times without penalty.
4. The official who takes his position above the top level of the net is _____.
5. Screening is an attempt by players to conceal the _____.
6. A volleyball match consists of the best _____.
7. In making a block the hands are tilted slightly _____.
8. The most popular offensive formation in competitive volleyball is the _____.
9. Volleyball was invented in _____.
10. Requests for substitutions may be made only by the _____ or _____.

9 BIBLIOGRAPHY

BOOKS

Emery, Curtis Ray. *Modern Volleyball*. New York: The Macmillan Co., 1953.

> This book presents volleyball fundamentals and major trends in the sport. It is an excellent reference and textbook.

Laveaga, Robert E. *Volleyball*. New York: Ronald Press Company, 1960.

> Fundamentals; good teaching devices for teams. General information.

Walters, M. L., ed. *Official Volleyball Guide*. Berne, Indiana: United States Volleyball Association, published annually.

> Rule book and guide.

Welch, J. Edmund, ed. *How To Play and Teach Volleyball*. New York: Association Press, 1960.

> Each chapter on fundamentals written by a different author.

ARTICLES

Bennett, Bruce L. "A Method of Improving Volleyball Team Play," *Journal of Health, Physical Education, and Recreation*, March 1947.

Caldwell, Web. "How To Serve," *International Volleyball Review*, November–December 1950.

Friermood, Harold T. "Volleyball Goes Modern," *Journal of Health, Physical Education, and Recreation*, May 1953.

Langston, Dewey F. "Standardization of a Volleyball Knowledge Test for College Physical Education Majors," *Research Quarterly*, March 1955.

Laveaga, Robert. "Making the Pass Effective," *International Volleyball Review*, January–February 1954.

Morgan, William. "How Volleyball Was Originated," *Official Volleyball Rules*. New York: American Sports Publishing Co., 1916.

Odeneal, William T. "Conditioning for Volleyball," *The Athletic Journal*, 1950.

——————. "Offensive Volleyball," *Scholastic Coach*, November 1954.

——————. "Volleyball—Major Sport," *Journal of Health, Physical Education, and Recreation*, January 1954.

——————. "Program for Volleyball Instruction," *Athletic Journal*, March 1951.

——————. "Volleyball Fundamentals," *Scholastic Coach*, March 1950.

——————. "Competitive Volleyball Drills," *Scholastic Coach*, April 1951.

——————. "Teamwork in Volleyball," *Journal of Health, Physical Education, and Recreation*, November 1957.

——————. "Defensive Volleyball Tactics," *Scholastic Coach*, November 1955.

Welch, J. Edmund. "Techniques of Officiating Volleyball," *Journal of Physical Education*, September–October 1953.

Wickstrom, Ralph L. "How To Teach the Underhand Pass in Volleyball," *Journal of Health, Physical Education, and Recreation*, January 1959.

BULLETINS

Bush, Wayne R. *Volleyball Class Drills*. Harrisburg, Pennsylvania, YMCA.

A description of drills for serving, passing, and spiking.

Emery, Curtis R. *Volleyball Fundamentals*, an *Athletic Journal* Feature, No. 6. Akron, Ohio: Pennsylvania Athletic Products.

Pictures of players passing, spiking, and digging the ball, with brief descriptions.

Lu, Hui Ching. "Volleyball Around the World" (Doctoral dissertation). New York: Teachers College, Columbia University, 1950.

A comprehensive study of volleyball, its history, and the supporting organizations in every country around the world.

Odeneal, William T. *Syllabus for Beginning Volleyball*. Tallahassee, Florida: Florida State University.

Lesson plans for forty-five college classes in Physical Education.

FILMS *

Beginning Volleyball. The Athletic Institute, 209 State Street, Chicago 4, Illinois. (Slide film—color, sound, 800-foot reel.) Instructor and student manuals also available. Robert E. Laveaga, Consultant.

Fundamentals of Volleyball—1959 Edition. 600 Long Beach Blvd., Long Beach 12, California. (Motion picture—black and white, sound, 400-foot reel.) Produced by Alton W. Fish and Dr. George B. Pearson.

Fun Playing Volleyball. Marjorie E. Fish, 1723 Oak Street, Orange Gardens, Kissimmee, Florida. (Motion picture—black and white or color.)

1955 National Volleyball Championships. Iowa Girls High School Athletic Union, Securities Building, Des Moines, Iowa. (Motion picture—black and white, sound.)

1957 National Volleyball Championships. William T. Odeneal, Florida State University, Tallahassee, Florida. (Motion picture—black and white, silent, 400-foot reel.)

Play Volleyball. Association Films, Inc., 35 West 45th Street, New York 19, New York. (Motion picture—black and white, sound, 400-foot reel.) Produced 1945.

Practice Makes Perfect. All American Productions, P.O. Box 801, Riverside, California. (Motion picture—black and white, sound, 400-foot reel.) Produced 1960.

Techniques in Volleyball for Girls. Scholastic Coach, 200 East 42nd Street, New York, New York. (Motion picture—black and white, silent, 400-foot reel.) Produced 1941.

Volleyball for Boys. Coronet Instructional Films, Palmolive Building, Chicago 11, Illinois. (Motion picture—black and white, sound, 400-foot reel.) Produced 1943.

* Rental fees and purchase prices for these films can be obtained from the individuals or organizations listed.

NOTES